Rest Upon the Flood

Rich Appel

REST UPON THE FLOOD

Copyright © 2024 Rich Appel

All Rights Reserved.

Published by Unsolicited Press.

First Edition.

For information contact:

Unsolicited Press

Portland, Oregon

www.unsolicitedpress.com

orders@unsolicitedpress.com

619-354-8005

Cover Design: Kathryn Gerhardt

Editor: S.R. Stewart

ISBN: 978-1-963115-05-5

For Adele & Fran

I wake to sleep, and take my waking slow.
I feel my fate in what I cannot fear.
I learn by going where I have to go.

Theodore Roethke
The Waking

Contents

III

Rest Upon The Flood

I

Ode

To my older cousin

who, outside Nick's Roast Beef at 20th and Jackson,

taught me the word *dickhead,*

and gave me a way of existing in the world of men

when I needed one:

pale and scrawny, naked,

goose-fleshed as a plucked chicken, and stranded

in the savage universe of puberty

where wild jockstraps soared across

the steamy skies of locker rooms,

everybody falling back laughing

at jokes I didn't understand.

But *dickhead* this and *dickhead* that,

a song that

meant the world

was mine enough at least

to bang on like a garbage can,

and knowing it, and having that

beautiful ugliness always

cocked and loaded in my mind,

protected me and calmed me and shaped me

like a psalm.

Prayer

Dark rain at winter solstice,

and in the morning, rosemary under clear sky.

A bird on south doorstep poised

like religion.

Let our words

be bright animals,

that fish

on a gull's wing.

If we pretend

that we are at the center, that moles and kingfishers,

eels and coyotes

are at the edge of grace,

then we circle, dead moons

about a cold sun.

This morning I ask only

the blessing of the crayfish, the beatitude of the birds;

to wear the skin of the bear

in our songs;

to work like a man,

to work like a woman,

with my hands.

Listings of the Heart

I tried to make a list of things I have

to remember, and a list

of things I want

to forget, but found them

both the same, and so

instead, scratched down

only what I'd need,

love and water on one side,

on the other the small flowers

that bloom without scent,

separated like this,

the way my grandmother

mapped out grocery lists,

milk and butter on one side,

meat on the other,

as if they shouldn't mingle

even on the page,

or how my mother, too, made lists

on tiny scraps of paper left on chairs

or the seats of the bus

the way one drops a handkerchief

for another to find, a clue,

a kind of commerce between her

and the world,

and all the while the tree

is making its endless list

of leaves; the sky

is listing its valuables

in rain.

Because

Because the night you asked me,
the small scar of the quarter moon
had healed—the moon was whole again;
because life seemed so short;
because life stretched before me
because I knew exactly what I wanted;
because I knew exactly nothing;
because I shed my childhood with my clothes—
they both had years of wear left in them;
because your eyes were darker than my mother's;
because my father said I could do better;
because I wanted badly to say no;
because Stanley Kowalski shouted *Stella…*;
because you were a door I could slam shut;
because endings are written before beginnings;
because I knew you'd bring the plants inside for winter
and make a jungle we'd sleep in naked;
because I had free will;
because everything is ordained;
I said yes.

The Bad Muse

Calm down. No one's listening. Of course,
most of it is done already.
Someone in New York or California
is writing the important poem about history
at this very moment.
And this person
has had a life of great interest,
full of struggle and incident, whereas yours
is the same old life a thousand people
have had the good sense to keep to themselves.
Who wants to hear about what it was like
to turn sixty, or the strange thing
your cats did last week? So relax.
Think of how good it will feel
to climb into bed and turn off the light.
And tomorrow is Sunday. You can read the papers,
go for a walk, cook outside. Friends will drop by,
Why not invite them all to stay for dinner?
And when conversation gets really lively
and they're nodding in agreement

with everything you say, maybe someone

will ask you to tell that story—you know,

the one about your grandfather

and the hundred ears of corn.

*To Morris Cohen, Who, in 1969, Sat On His Front Stoop
in West Philly And Mocked This Very Art Form I Would
Later Come to Need*

No poem ever bought a hamburger, it's true,

and no, these walls are not tight, windows

open at night to the rain, to the songs of stars

muffled by distance. But

every moment lasts eternally, becomes

a point, a haven, an envelope of emotion,

every thought is a light coin

which rolls its shy secretive being

into a song, into a dance,

into a painting, a poem.

Every joy, even the non-existent one, leaves

a transparent trace. Frost kisses

the pane because it can't get into the room.

It is not the moon, I tell you:

it is these flowers lighting the yard,

illuminating the unfinished house.

Mr. Cohen, fifty years later,

and I am still in silence:

no answers,

no advice,

no cures.

But the sounds of words

carry what we do not.

For what are we rich enough,

And for whom?

Musing

A black page of night

flutters: dream on or waken,

words will spring from darkness now,

gold-bright, to fill the hollow mind

laid still to hear them, as the iron cup

laid on the window ledge, would fill with rain.

Learning How to Write

It's cold outside, or it's dark.

It's raining, or it could be.

Why not begin with that?

In the bright sun, the trees

are perfectly still,

which only a moment ago thrashed about

in the storm.

The sky is a sheet of blue paper,

which may lead to an ocean or sorrow.

There are streets and pathways

and people stroll along them.

Or just yourself. Or your father.

It's years ago and he's happy

having learned he's becoming your father.

Things show up,

and you gather them together,

things that look like anything

that might be from around here.

Now you're walking home from school,

the day the dog chased you

into the street and the car

hit you. And it's possible now

to see the funeral, your small coffin

the way they lower it so carefully,

the way they don't start

shoveling the dirt on top of you

until the family has left.

It's cold outside and it's dark.

But you can follow them home, you can be

a ghost in the corner of your own room,

and at night you can listen and find out

how much they really miss you.

And after you've heard enough

you might decide to be back

in your body, waiting on the corner by the curb,

so when the dog comes out

you are ready with a stick

you've given yourself, except

this time maybe it should be raining,

not hard but steadily, and all the cars

are moving very slowly and very carefully

since at any moment and for no reason

someone might run out there.

Outer Banks, Too

For my son, Ben

Here is a child who presses his head to the ground

his eyes open

he sees through one window

the flat gray ocean

upside down with an arbor of islands hanging from it

all the way to the horizon

and he himself is hanging from nothing

he might step down

and walk on the old sky far down there

out to the clouds

in the far islands

he might step on the clouds where they have worn shiny

he might jump from cloud to cloud

he watches lights flash

on and off along the darkening shores

and the lights moving among the overhead islands

he feels his head like a boat on a beach

he heard the waves break around his ears

he stands up and listens

he turns to a room full of his elders

with the lights on

and without moving

he flies.

Monster Truck Show

My nine-year-old son could care less about Miss Monster Jam
waving from the pickup bed in blue sequins,
or the chrome parade of new Fords for '08.
He wants the monster trucks: Big Foot, Crusher, Grave Digger
to prowl and splash thick mud,
spread it like brown sugar over the arena's sod.
Their bodies sit high atop fat tires,
tiny afterthoughts of control
over naked, unmuffled engines,
coiled springs, and black axles
bulging like snakes that swallowed whole pigs.
The announcer intones *the incredible war*
between Taurus and Big Foot;
both drivers prove that *nothing*
will ever knock this country
from the #1 spot.
I'm edgy when a dad
puts shooting-range ear muffs on his son's head,
while Taurus creeps to the starting line,
a deafening, guttural roar slingshotting truck

from muddy mist, arcing over flattened cars,

wheels gyrating, slamming the mud,

sliding to a stop. Ben's fingers grip my thigh.
His open-mouthed gaze

focuses on the inner dome of the arena.

He's seen only TV ads,

and now his fears reverberate

from every ghostly rafter.

I say fatherly things:
It's only engine noise; Look, that kid likes it.

He knows he asked to come,

but each roar touches some fathom of nerves.

On my lap he pops Pez and drinks Sprite

until the sixth truck leaps, and finally,

in all the adult tones he can muster, says,
It's time to go now.

The Crusher growls as we scurry up the steps,

ducking into the bathroom door labeled *Men*, cringing

as another roar fills the upper decks.

He's near tears now.

Pushing through an exit,

the quiet, cold city air drags us past long trailers

with Day-Glo pictures of the trucks,

Taurus' caricature getting his bull teeth,

horns smoking

like belching factory stacks

in an old political cartoon of capitalism.

Lingering under its wake of airbrushed lines,

There is now another voice,

a big man shivers in rags

behind an outstretched hand,

bulbous purple scars know the finger joints---

Help me get back to the shelter. I'm broke.

Been sleeping under a bridge.

My son Ben leans behind my leg,

peeking at the crooked knuckles.

Menace, imagined or real,

mixes with his pained growl

hanging over us both.

I think of the roaring trucks,

vaulting over crushed cars

again and again,

the raucous cheers with each leap.

I reach in my pocket.

Intro his hand I drop

all my change.

Middle Age

Having somehow survived the traumas
of growth, of passing
from school life to *life* life,
the job, the marriage, the suburbs,
mortgages, adoption,
toilet training, playgroups,
you arrive here,
dressed for an afternoon
when for the first time since what seems like forever,
they've all disappeared
to one place or another, leaving you
on your own for the moment,
and after you've relished the quiet luxury
of having nothing immediate to do
spreading out around you,
you find that you're really not quite sure what to do
with yourself,
suddenly picturing your mother sitting up
alone in the front porch darkness, cigarette flaring,
so you shake yourself and go down

to the basement to dust off the guitar,

but the notes have gone stiff,

so you come back up

and try some Dostoyevsky

you haven't read since college,

but your margined notes

are incomprehensible now,

so you put on an old Oscar Peterson record,

but it's fuzzy and scratched and repeats

and repeats and repeats,

and by now you're in no mood

to attack that set of exams

you should've done over the weekend,

or tangle with the new poem

that seemed hopelessly

snarled this morning, and so,

for the moment, defeated,

you just sit still,

at a loss, alone,

in the living room, drowning in silence,

a bit scared, resentful, and sorry

for yourself, because here you are,

after all these years,

having made it through in one piece

[if not with flying colors]

to middle age, suddenly free at last,

and nobody's handing out stars,

or calling up to ask if you can come out

after dinner to play.

Haiku

My scrotum blossomed.
Stranded alone in Times Square,
Acid's wearing off.

II

A Sensualist Speaks on Faith

Smile like fingers on their way
toward the cold, curved doorknob.
If you walk through a spider web,
pity those who miss the flamboyant
tapestry of everything floating
beyond the silky string.

If you lie down with words that are ugly,
close your eyes, imagine
a time when no one was
guilty or clever.
Inhale deeply, again
and again, and in that breathing
hear the wordless faith
of our first ancestors—
the ones who forgave
their fins and swam to shore,
the ones who didn't question
the ache of a beginning
made on sand.

Considering My Words

Already, thirty-three years have elapsed
since I went from student to teacher.
Since then, happy and unhappy,
each day I have talked to myself, seriously,
of the value of life, the nature of good,
my own shortcomings, the illusions of time,
the hatreds of men and women,
and other notions, abstract or otherwise.
I have often had to pick from my hair and collar
the leaves which fell there
while I was lost in thought.
No doubt regret is the price I pay
for these conversations, but do not pity me.
Everyone I ever loved, I still love.
It is true that my terrain is ignorance,
that often I lean against this tree in exhaustion,
that solace is as close as I may ever come to goodness.
Yet one must not underestimate the pleasures
of clear thought and clear words
when each must appear out of night and nothingness
as elsewhere, rocks emerge from morning fog.

A Course in Creative Writing

Day after day up there beating my wings
with all of the softness truth requires,
I feel them shrug whenever I pause:
they class my voice among tentative things.
And they credit fact, force, battering.
I dance my way toward that family of knowing,
embracing stray error as a long-lost girl
and bringing her home with my fluttering.
They want a wilderness with a map—
but how about errors that give a new start?—
or leaves that are edging into the light?—
or the many places a road can't find?
Or maybe there's a land where you have to sing
to explain anything: you blow a little whistle
just right and the next tree you meet is itself.
Things come toward you when you walk.
You go along singing a song that says
where you are going becomes its own
because you start. You blow a little whistle—
And a world begins under the map.

Notice

It is time to notice, I say, the freezing snow
hesitating toward us from its gray heaven;
listen—
it is falling not quite silently
and under it still, you
and I are walking.

Maybe there are trumpets
in the houses we pass, a red bird
watching from an evergreen.

Nothing will happen
until we pause
to flame what we know.
No signal with be given.

They Call This a Table

In her joy to be alive,

the woman put her keys on the table;

she put some flowers in the copper bowl;

put her milk and eggs;

put the light from the window;

the woman put the softness of bread and of air

on the table;

she put the events in her mind;

whatever she wanted to do in life,

she put that on the table;

those she loved, those she didn't love,

the woman put them on the table too;

three times three make nine,

so, the woman put the nine on the table;

the window was nearby; the sky next to her;

leaning across, she put endlessness on the table;

for several days she had craved a beer;

on the table she put the outpouring;

she put her sleep;

put her wakefulness;

put her hunger and her fullness.

They call this a table.

It raised no fuss under so much weight,

swaying once or twice;

meanwhile, the woman kept putting;

the woman kept putting.

Folk Song

First no sound, then you hear it—

so Sally, so Tom:

it's the past, its wisdom,

quick in the head again,

back then when the moon climbed home

and someone began the song,

we were a people together

alive in the dark.

Now, puzzle it with notes for a while,

shake it over the land:

this is your country, broken,

and broken and broken.

Sing it together 'til you hold it—

all Sally, all Tom:

make our time, its promise,

come true in the air again.

Primal Song

The other world's not for me—
no, I'll let my dead stroll
that pale road, pale throat,
each of its pebbles,
white and vanishing.

I far prefer minnow
and sunnies. I need
to know what mouths know:
round stone in a stream,
heart buried in a box, to fetch
what's down there, black
and cold as a lump of coal.

To go that deep: ash and tear,
but to come back up: bud and leaf.

Want

All these yearnings,

faces, rooms, books left open,

everything bearing our names,

appearing even in dreams

always in disguise, but

so real that we wake

each day, sore-armed

from our nighttime reaching,

remembering little but

the taste of desire

that lingers all day,

as an animal there

under the table,

as the stars are there

even in full sun.

Never Alone

Here is the sound of footfall in snow,

the absence of birds,

all of this stillness. Listen,

the whispering inside,

that feeling, *never alone,*

a frozen log broken

free from the woodpile,

the sound of perfect inhumanity

bouncing all through the valley

like the airy call of crows

at the darker end of twilight,

awakening me

in the middle of life. So sweet,

this night. No moon, but urgent

stars.

I am acutely here.

Everyone is somewhere else.

Wonderings

Might people stumble and wander
for not knowing the right words,
and get lost in their wanderings?
Can your words
link especially to some other stranger?
Should you stand in the street
answering all passwords
day and night for any stranger?
Can a package of passwords
bring strangers together?
Can it offer light that goes forth looking for the eye?
Can it mark tears that clarify the eye toward charity?
Can it praise loss, its particular weights, its music?

Saying Goodbye to Any Poetry Class

As you head out, notice the trash can by the door,

open to whatever you like to leave—

these claims you accepted for a while

from the louder, forceful voices

but not really your cup of tea, those heavy opinions

balanced up on such fragile foundations.

We invite you to retain your tickets for noticing

how sunlight is wide and democratic, how

the rain doesn't care who you are,

all those sounds following you home

to become songs that play back when you need them.

A crow, a gull, a foghorn—keep them

for your dreams.

Haiku

My scrotum blossomed.
But I miss you desperately.
---Cell phone on vibrate.

III

Prime Numbers

For Soren

Prime numbers, I remember them
like five drinks following one friend's shooting.
Out in California
another friend visits a pebble
beach, indivisible
in that uncertain life.

Elegy

The strong leaves of the box elder tree,

plunging in the wind, call us to disappear

into the wilds of the universe,

where we shall sit at the foot of a plant,

and live forever, like the dust.

Voices Above, Voices Below

I

Honks above in the growing dark,

the feathered bundles tight,

beak to foot,

calling out again and again

to keep track, keep pace,

so that none forgets itself,

so that none is lost.

II

Picture us by the sea,

skin and sun and sweat,

hoping, maybe, for touch, for talk,

all the while the water,

eye of the earth, observing,

sending little messages,

return

be at rest.

Prologue Before Meditation

Admit the sky carries no threatening message

to cloud or color. The birds wing by,

the only disturbance and pleasure.

The grass gives you gentleness and the earth selflessness.

You are encouraged on all sides by the impersonal.

Admit: the grasshopper sways upon a blade.

Men rest themselves upon the flood.

Rock Face: A Lesson in Stone

Teach me
to be like you, to take
a beating and keep
my mouth shut,

to settle,

to carry the sun
in my stomach
deep into the night.

Mist: A Dedication to Surrealism

I

Today forty tongues
are hiding in the trees
their voices are hanging beyond the mist
forty long banners mingling
red yellow
blue voices
hanging silent
here the nuthatch blows his horn
leading a thin procession of white wind
past the black trees
through the world.

II

Years from now
someone will come upon a layer of birds
and not know what he is listening for

these are mists

where the beetles hurry through dry grass

hiding pieces of light they have stolen.

Loyalty

Some people, they tire of their dogs
and each other, they get a divorce.
Their car breaks down, they trade it in.
A sweater gets a hole in the elbow,
they throw it away.

I take thee, Rover, for better or worse,
in sickness and in health, for richer,
for poorer, till death do us part.

The White Cracker-Barrow

For William Carlos Williams

So much depends

upon a burnt flapjack

glazed with Karo syrup

beside the white Caucasians.

In Memory of My Liver

The first put back is for the song
they always play in this dive,
and of course you know it,
all whoop-stomps and whatever the hell else,
before another with its sweat
making lakes of the table carvings
(lovers names in hearts and the obligatory dick).
Then next goes down for the thirst,
the tune we can't remember but still whistle, god damnit,
like waking from dreams we keep
just for ourselves,
or the body's dogs, lying at home
by the ashtray and thumping
around in their sleep.
And while we're at it, a round
for whoever goes home and sprawls,
like the rogue sock, naked of course,
on the floor so close to the bed.
And fuck it.
One for the road and the traffic

traveling on its tongue of light

all the way back home.

Imagination is Good Wood

Even as the last bars clang shut
and I start to rub the purple ache
clubs left on my shoulders, ribs
and shins, my mind is fashioning
an invisible ladder, its rungs
and lifts of escape.
Imagination is good wood; by midnight
I'll be as high as that mockingbird
in the magnolia across the moonlit road.
Some days we need to be given back to ourselves
like an unexpected present, to be remembered
not as we are now, but as we were
before the wheel took its turn with us,
and the notches began to appear like clockwork
around our eyes and carved into our foreheads.

Proposition

After Francis Daulerio's *Joy*

Come,
let flowers bloom in every heart,
heads bent to breathe in the scent
of life: a world of growers,
abundant blooms and pockets stuffed,
arms outstretched, to rally, to hold,
some light shoved under your door.

Am I dreaming?

Worry

For Bobby McFerrin

My friends, the worriers make themselves miserable,

I suppose, in preparation for the misery to come.

They must be practicing for the time lightning will destroy

their homes, or for when their spouses die

on a fog-plagued strip of road. Bird flu

and if their hotel room will be too close to the ice machine

often begin to live side by side in their minds.

They can't help it, they say, these servants of catastrophe,

often adding that I seem to suffer from under-worry,

which causes them to worry for and about me the more.

And so, since worry always trumps the absence of worry,

to live with them is to live on their terms. Don't worry

I've learned not to say, which is other-planetary language

to them, cold, unsympathetic, the language of someone

who wouldn't help them build a bomb shelter

after they seen the end of the world in a dream.

Try to be reasonable, is the button that triggers the bomb.

I try to love them for their other qualities,

like being right about most other things, or how good

they are in in kitchen, or the workplace, or the bed.

But if not for my sake, then for their own: shouldn't
they worry less, or at least privately? Every once in a while,

shouldn't they say: "Forgive me my worries?"

But a semi is always running a stop sign,

one of the big hemlocks topples in a storm.

Then they point to the gasping state of World News

or Public Education. What's wrong with you,

they want to know?

Don't you know what's out there?

A failure of imagination they say.

A man who's a clear danger to himself.

Ode to the Last Hippie, Heading Out

Beyond here there's no map.
How you get there is where
you'll arrive; how, dawn by
dawn, you can see your way
clear: in ponds, sky, just as
woods you walk through give
to fields. And rivers: beyond
all burning, you'll cross on bridges
you've lugged with you.
Whatever your route, go lightly
toward light. Once you give away
all save necessity, all's
mostly well: what you used to
believe you owned is nothing,
nothing beside how you've come
to feel. You've no need now
to give in or give out: the way
you're going your body seems
willing. Slowly as it may

otherwise tell you, whatever

it comes to, you're bound to know.

Notes

The poem "Ode" was eventually published by Westwind: A UCLA
Journal of the Arts, Winter 2020 in what they called "The Lost
Issue" due to the restrictions of the Pandemic.

The epigraph at the beginning of the collection was taken from
Theodore Roethke's *"The Waking"* originally published in *The
Collected Poems of Theodore Roethke,* Anchor Books, 1975.

Acknowledgments

Many people—whether they know it or not—enabled me to write this book. First, it was my wife Adele, who provided me with a lifetime of unwavering love and support which essentially fostered my foundation of emotional well-being and security. Your gift of love each day has provided me with a level of joy, happiness, and kindness that I had never imagined would come my way in life. Thank you for sharing your life with me.

Second, any success in completing this book of poems was due to my friend and fellow poet Fran Daulerio, and his great skill in providing spot-on feedback and editing suggestions to my words. Every writer needs a reader who will embrace your words. He became the catalyst to clarify my ideas and made it easier for the reader to walk with me on my journey. Thanks for sharing in this heavy lifting; your feedback, embracing the sound and sense of my words, was always a gift that is incalculable.

Third, I owe a large debt of thanks to my writing group of poets, especially to fellow poet Dorothy Brown, whose poetry I always admired and whose friendship and close reading over these many years helped foster my writing and clarify my ideas. Writers, like comedians, need a place to be bad and then learn how to develop their craft, and my writing group provided that place for me over many years. Thanks for adopting me. Thanks for your words.

Four, I also owe a debt of thanks to my friend, Russ Frank, who is now a journalist professor at Penn State, but, who in our younger years was a graduate student with me at UCLA; there he shared his poetry and his paper on romantic poetry written in his younger years, before he became an accomplished journalist and folklorist both in California and Pennsylvania. These texts were studied and opened up possibilities for finding my own voice. Thanks for your ongoing friendship all these years. I am always amazed by your great gift for words.

Last, the journey for writing poetry began accidentally at Penn State when I was 17, when I had met older students who were actively working to become poets themselves. Loving what they were writing, as well as wanting to desperately fit in with these older, more mature students (they all had girlfriends too!), I began writing poems in the hopes of being accepted. Well, my early poems were quite horrific, but my new friends never laughed at them, at least not to my face; instead, they always encouraged me to continue writing as a way to improve. They were my first teachers (i.e. encouragers) in the process of learning how to write. I give thanks to these fellow poets who really awakened the passion in me, which has only grown exponentially in all these years.

About the Author

After a succession of meaningless jobs (busboy, waiter, camp counselor, etc.), Rich Appel worked in Grey's Ferry in South Philadelphia as a social worker and community organizer for five years, before studying Folklore and Mythology at UCLA. Rich has received three National Endowment for the Humanities Fellowship Awards for Teachers, and worked as an eleventh and twelfth grade English teacher for over thirty years. He also is an adjunct at Delaware County Community College teaching freshman English. He has been writing poetry since undergraduate school at Penn State University, where he first met older, more accomplished writers who never laughed at the bad poetry he'd first written.

About the Press

Unsolicited Press is based out of Portland, Oregon and focuses on the works of the unsung and underrepresented. As a womxn-owned, all-volunteer small publisher that doesn't worry about profits as much as championing exceptional literature, we have the privilege of partnering with authors skirting the fringes of the lit world. We've worked with emerging and award-winning authors such as Frances Daulerio, Shann Ray, Heather Lang-Cassera, Amy Shimshon-Santo, Brook Bhagat, Kris Amos, and John W. Bateman.

Learn more at unsolicitedpress.com. Find us on twitter and instagram.

www.ingramcontent.com/pod-product-compliance
Lightning Source LLC
Chambersburg PA
CBHW031251120626
46545CB00007B/2751